BEAUTIFUL LONDON

PHAIDON

ST. PAUL'S CATHEDRAL: THE NORTH-WEST TOWER

BEAUTIFUL
LONDON

103 PHOTOGRAPHS BY

HELMUT GERNSHEIM

WITH A FOREWORD BY

JAMES POPE-HENNESSY

PHAIDON PRESS · LONDON

MADE IN GREAT BRITAIN 1960
PLATES PRINTED BY CLARKE & SHERWELL LTD., NORTHAMPTON
TEXT PRINTED BY GEO. GIBBONS LTD., LEICESTER

FOREWORD

BY JAMES POPE-HENNESSY

T HE LARGEST CAPITAL in the world, London is a city which was never planned. It has accumulated. For this reason, and also because its development was chiefly guided by mercantile considerations, London is no longer, at first sight, overtly beautiful. Haphazard and shapeless, it offers few fine vistas and has no kind of symmetry. Its component boroughs seem self-contained and unrelated to each other, for once beyond the ancient boundaries of the City proper, and once outside the Government quarter of Westminster and Whitehall, London is nothing but a mass of rural villages — Kensington, Tottenham, Paddington, Camberwell, Edmonton, Hampstead and so on — engulfed in the tide of two centuries of swift urban expansion. Even Westminster itself was long a separate entity, an Abbey church and royal palace standing high across the water-meadows, accessible to Londoners by river. At one time, as Canaletto shows us, London's finest visual asset, the appearance of this river has been allowed to degenerate since the demolition of the great waterside palaces of the Tudor and Stuart nobility, until, murky, much narrowed, and held in by drab embankments of Victorian granite, the Thames in London is now only beautiful at certain times of day, in certain lights, from certain viewpoints — from Waterloo Bridge at dawn or on a summer's evening for example, and at night from Cardinals' Wharf on the South Bank, or from the water-stairs down in Wapping where the Thames looks as alien and mysterious as the Maas at Rotterdam. In 1951 the Exhibition buildings for the Festival of Britain may do something to alleviate the dreary aspect of the Thames' South Bank; but such alleviation, in its essence temporary, is too local and too late to restore to the London river that lost spaciousness and splendour that once made it rival the Paris Seine.

It is certain that the stranger — English or foreign — must be initially bewildered by his first sight of London; it is not unlikely that he may also be disappointed or repelled. It will seem noisy and inchoate, over-crowded, over-large, and filled with undisciplined-looking buildings, many of them — Caxton Hall, Albert Hall Mansions, the Hotel Russell — in more than dubious taste. But, though we cannot claim for it the immediate fascination of Paris, nor Dublin's tired charm, nor the stinging stimulus of New York's first impact, nor even such a situation as that of the capital town of Oslo at the head of the fjord, this city contains not only a number of architectural works of the first importance, but a myriad places of quiet, rather melancholy beauty, as well as many hundreds with historical and literary associations for students and lovers of the past. The architectural beauties of London are most often unexpected. They are sometimes hard to find. Not many people know that if you push open the high forbidding wooden gates of the Deanery at St. Paul's, you will find yourself standing in a moss-grown courtyard made dark by plane trees, and facing the dim front of a brick town-house by Sir Christopher Wren. One can wager that many, many Londoners have never seen the sphinxes in Chiswick Park, the Tudor tombs at Stoke Newington, the splendid Norman pillars of Waltham Abbey, the Geffryes workhouses at Shoreditch, the small street sloping down to Saint-Andrew-by-the-Wardrobe, the Italian villas on the Paddington Canal, the little graveyard, feathery with sheep's parsley in summertime, of the Old Church at Edmonton where Charles Lamb lies buried, or that oddest of all Victorian funeral schemes, the Catacombs and Columbarium in Highgate Cemetery, here photographed for the first time. It is such places as these, together with some more well-known London scenes, that have been caught by the discriminating camera of Mr. Helmut Gernsheim. A selection from these photographs, in which the beauty of London is the theme consistently emphasized, has here been assembled.

ROYAL NAVAL COLLEGE, GREENWICH: STUCCO ORNAMENTATION IN THE CHAPEL

HAMPTON COURT PALACE, THE GREAT HALL: FAN-VAULTED CEILING OVER THE DAIS

It is safe to say that the three most famous buildings in England are Westminster Abbey, the Tower of London and St. Paul's Cathedral. In spite of Henry VII's chapel, the Abbey is not, in its exterior, a very inspired nor in any way a major example of English Gothic; it is the Abbey's rich contents, the tomb-figures ranging from the gilt-bronze kings and queens of Plantagenet England, with their tapering fingers and sublime features, and the Torrigiano tomb of the first Tudor, to the gesticulating figures of Roubiliac, that make each visit to it so rewarding. Seen across Parliament Square, the Abbey looks overshadowed by its neo-Gothic neighbour, the New Palace of Westminster. It does not stand out. The outlines of the Tower and St. Paul's, on the other hand, loom along the river, two silhouettes which have come to represent London to people all over the world. The area which these two buildings together dominate — the area of the City, from Blackfriars to Tower Hill — is one in which the feel of old London has lingered longest. In atmosphere the City might be loosely termed 'Dickensian' but the names of the streets and alleys and wharfs, the names of the churches above all, take one back to the Middle Ages, and to the days before the Great Fire. Like those aged Roman cities of Provence, which still preserve some feeling that is classical and pagan, though all but a few crumbling monuments of Antiquity have gone, the City of London, scourged by fire in 1666, by bombs in 1940, suffering in the last century from such pieces of vandalism as the sale and deliberate demolition of some of Wren's churches by the Bishop of London, by day an inferno of petrol fumes and scurrying office workers, takes on an almost medieval immobility by night. When the typists have been drained away to the suburbs by the Underground, and the offices and churches stand locked and silent, the City of London assumes a timeless quality. The Royal Exchange, the Bank of England and the Mansion House stand impassively in the deserted City, white and remote as a group of tombs and temples beside the moonlit Nile. The steeples of Wren's churches rise white and slender into the evening air above the rooftops, or show clearly across the jungle of bomb damage thick with weeds and where you may trace the twisting patterns of the old lanes. In contrast to these white spires the column of the Monument looks black; the fine bas-relief upon its base showing the rebuilding of London after 1666 is sooty too, and damaged by bomb splinters; under the porch of the neighbouring church of St. Magnus the Martyr, and on the stairs that lead up to the road level of London Bridge, the shadows are as black as ink. At the back of the Monument (down Fish Street Hill, which still smells as it did when Shakespeare mentions it in Henry VI), the grilles of Billingsgate Market are shut. Thronged each day by the yelling fish-porters, who still wear their circular hats of wood and boiled leather, the form of which dates from the time of Fouquet, the market offers you at night a shining perspective of empty caverns with liquid floors, the only occupant a famished cat crouched over a shattered fish-crate, gnawing noiselessly. If you pursue your way down Lower Thames Street, you come at length upon the ruined church, All Hallows Barking, and the Tower. Long, low, irregular, protected by a broad ditch and crouched behind casemate walls, the Tower of London looks sinister by night. A stray light may be glimmering through a mullion window, or in some turret. An ugly war-memorial obscures your vision of the scaffold site outside the walls, on Tower Hill.

In the same way, you can, if you choose, wander across to Smithfield, under the solid thirteenth-century gateway of St. John of Jerusalem, or past St. Bartholomew the Great, which since the destruction of the Austin Friars and All Hallows Barking in the last war, is one of the two survivors of the vast monastic churches that once adorned the medieval City. If you wish to see the tomb of Rahere, or to see anything else in these buildings, you must naturally go by day; but to get a strong impression of the romanticism lurking in the old City, there is no better way than to wander about after sundown, when the damp river air rises in your nostrils, when your heels echo on the pavements as though they were shod in copper, when the only human being about is a solitary police constable on his beat on one of the bridges, and the only sound of voices comes from some small and bright-lit pub.

Although succeeding generations have done many things to the interior of St. Paul's Cathedral which would have made Wren wince — the erection of the reredos, for example, and of the equestrian statue of the Duke of Wellington — the Cathedral is unquestionably the finest specimen of Renaissance church architecture in this country. As much as Westminster Abbey, St. Paul's repays a series of visits, for, as Mr. Gernsheim here persuades us, it contains many details which on a hurried visit one might miss. Serious visits to St. Paul's can and should be combined with others to Wren's numerous London churches. Out of eighty-nine lost in the Great Fire, he prepared plans to rebuild fifty-two; and, though some of these perished in the last war (when ten were burned out in a single night alone), a great many remain, and at least one that has been bombed is in the process of being reconditioned and restored. To extend one's study of this great London architect further, one need only go down river to Greenwich, or up river to Hampton Court. It is also interesting to look again at Wren's rearrangement of the old country house of Lord Northampton at Kensington, which he adapted as a palace for William the Third. This movement of the court towards Kensington (a village which had always been notable for its healthy air and seemed likely to do King William's asthma good) accounted for the sudden development of this country district as an urban residential area, and gave London its oldest surviving square, Kensington Square.

The creation of the area of London known today as the 'West End' — St. James's, Berkeley and Grosvenor Squares, the warren of Mayfair, the dignified squares and streets laid out upon the Cavendish estates north of Oxford Street — was, of course, an eighteenth-century achievement. The contemporary English public has only very recently been taught to appreciate Georgian architecture, and to unlearn the Victorian dislike of this graceful and urbane style. In the nineteen-twenties and 'thirties much that was most beautiful in the London architecture of this period was allowed to disappear — Berkeley Square, Chesterfield House, Lansdowne House, Dorchester House have gone; and in place of the great houses along the Park, we have the present vulgar blocks of big hotels, American in their conception but insufficiently so in their execution. The Adelphi too has gone, and many other buildings designed and decorated by the brothers Adam; though as Mr. Gernsheim shows we still have the Royal Society of Arts, and those elegant distinguished buildings housing the clubs of St. James's Street. The last productions of the Georgian style — the Athenaeum, for instance — are also fine; and the first onset of Victorianism, as demonstrated in Barry's Reform Club, his Traveller's Club, and his Bridgewater House, is in no way displeasing. The real disasters of London architecture began later in the century and for some of the worst — Charing Cross Hotel for instance — Barry's son Edward was responsible. By the 'sixties and 'seventies the rot had properly set in. Even Mr. Gernsheim's camera would be tested to find 'beauties' amongst the orange mansions of Pont Street, unwieldy and expensive buildings in the new 'Holbeinesque' style.

All through the nineteenth century, London was spreading. It was creeping outwards on all sides, down towards Chelsea, up to Highgate and Hampstead which it quickly swallowed in its maw. Owing to the preservation of the Heath these two places seem country towns rather than regions of London. Heath Street and Golden Yard are more like corners of Tewkesbury or Romsey than parts of a metropolis. Next to arriving in London by air at night, when it looks like a complete continent of lights, you can get the clearest sense of its immensity by standing on Hampstead Heath, and looking down across the leafy countryside to the city below. This is the view prettily described by James Thomson, a mid-Victorian, whose verse is similar in sentiment to the painting of Frith. *Sunday at Hampstead, 1863* concerns two young people who have escaped the desk and counter' in the great city below for a few hours:

> *This is the Heath of Hampstead,*
> *There is the dome of Saint Paul's;*
> *Beneath, on the serried housetops,*
> *A chequered lustre falls;*

And the mighty city of London,
Under the clouds and the light,
Seems a low wet beach, half shingle,
With a few sharp rocks upright.

Would you mind very much, my darling,
If all yon low wet shore
Were drowned by a mighty flood-tide
And we never toiled there more?

Since 1863, London, though it has avoided a 'flood-tide', has been exposed to dangers and undergone changes that would have appalled James Thomson's carefree boys and girls. But in spite of all that has been destroyed in one way or in another, by war, commercialism or stupidity, its essential character survives unaltered, as the photographs in this book testify.

THE PLATES

I. ST. PAUL'S CATHEDRAL FROM THE EAST

2. ST. PAUL'S CATHEDRAL: DECORATIVE SHELL WINDOW

3. ST. PAUL'S CATHEDRAL: CAPITAL OF DRUM GALLERY, AND CLOCK TOWER

4. ST. PAUL'S CATHEDRAL: SPIRAL STAIRCASE IN CLOCK TOWER, LOOKING UP

5. ST. PAUL'S CATHEDRAL: SPIRAL STAIRCASE IN CLOCK TOWER, LOOKING DOWN

6. ST. PAUL'S CATHEDRAL: LORD NELSON

7. ST. PAUL'S CATHEDRAL: UPPER GALLERY OF CLOCK TOWER

8. THE RUINS OF ST. MARY-LE-BOW

9.   THE CHURCH OF ST. MARY-LE-STRAND

IO. BURLINGTON HOUSE: THE ROYAL ACADEMY OF ARTS

11. SOMERSET HOUSE

12.   THE ROYAL SOCIETY OF ARTS, JOHN ADAM STREET, ADELPHI

13. OFFICES OF 'THE LANCET', ADAM STREET, ADELPHI

14. TRAFALGAR SQUARE: VIEW TOWARDS WESTMINSTER

15. TRAFALGAR SQUARE AND ST. MARTIN'S-IN-THE-FIELDS

16. THE NATIONAL GALLERY AND ST. MARTIN'S-IN-THE-FIELDS

17. TRAFALGAR SQUARE AND THE NATIONAL GALLERY

18. WATERLOO PLACE

19. THE ATHENAEUM CLUB, WATERLOO PLACE

20.   ST. JAMES'S PALACE: THE GATEHOUSE

21. ST. JAMES'S SQUARE, WITH STATUE OF WILLIAM III

22. BOODLE'S CLUB, ST. JAMES'S STREET

23. BROOKS'S CLUB, ST. JAMES'S STREET

24. ST. GEORGE'S CHURCH, HANOVER SQUARE

25. THE GROSVENOR CHAPEL, SOUTH AUDLEY STREET

26. THE WELLINGTON ARCH, GREEN PARK

27.   CARLTON HOUSE TERRACE, THE MALL

28. PICCADILLY CIRCUS

29. ROYAL HORSE GUARD, WHITEHALL

30. RELIEVING THE GUARD, BUCKINGHAM PALACE

31. NO. 10, DOWNING STREET

32.   BUCKINGHAM PALACE AND QUEEN VICTORIA MEMORIAL

33. THE ADMIRALTY, WHITEHALL

34. ST. JAMES'S PARK: VIEW TOWARDS WHITEHALL

35. LANCASTER HOUSE, GREEN PARK

36. HORSE GUARDS, WHITEHALL

37.   BIG BEN AND THE HOUSES OF PARLIAMENT

38. THE HOUSES OF PARLIAMENT, FROM THE ROOF OF HENRY VII'S CHAPEL, WESTMINSTER ABBEY

39. WESTMINSTER ABBEY: HENRY VII'S CHAPEL

40. WESTMINSTER ABBEY: HENRY III

41. WESTMINSTER ABBEY: EDWARD III

42. WESTMINSTER ABBEY: HANDS OF HENRY VII

43. WESTMINSTER ABBEY: HENRY VII

44. WESTMINSTER ABBEY: STAG AT THE FEET OF LADY MARGARET BEAUFORT, MOTHER OF HENRY VII

45. WESTMINSTER ABBEY: CHERUB FROM THE TOMB OF HENRY VII

46. WESTMINSTER ABBEY: SIR ISAAC NEWTON

47.   WESTMINSTER ABBEY: DETAIL OF THE NEWTON MONUMENT

48. WESTMINSTER ABBEY: DR. JOHNSON

49. WESTMINSTER ABBEY: HANDEL

50. WESTMINSTER ABBEY: THE LITTLE CLOISTERS

51. WESTMINSTER ABBEY: THE CLOISTERS

52. THREE THAMES BRIDGES: SOUTHWARK, CANNON STREET, AND LONDON BRIDGE

53 · THE EMBANKMENT

54A. GATE OF ST. BARTHOLOMEW THE GREAT

54B. THE OLD CURIOSITY SHOP

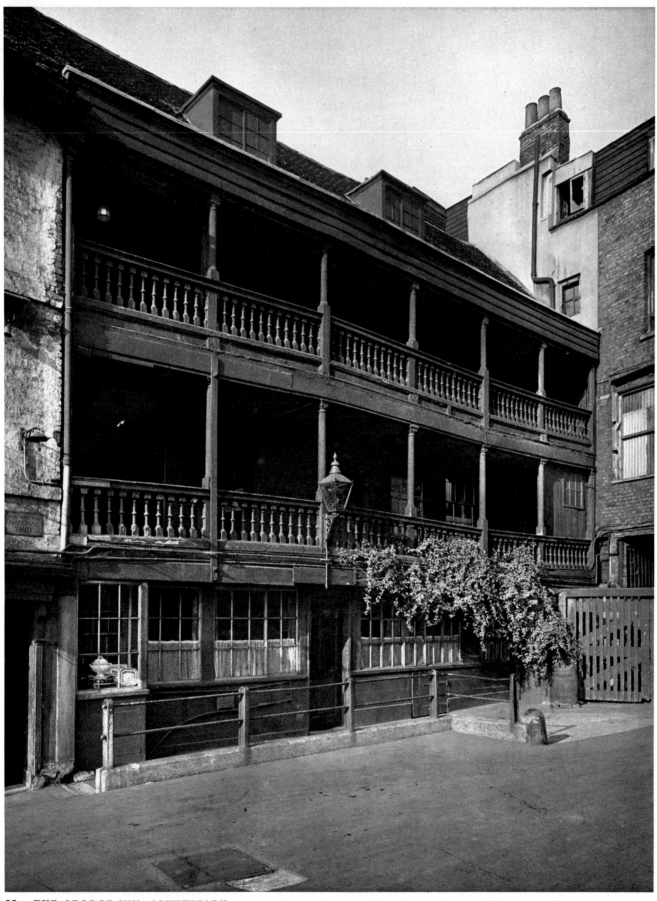

55. THE GEORGE INN, SOUTHWARK

56. ST. BARTHOLOMEW THE GREAT

57. GATE OF ST. BARTHOLOMEW'S HOSPITAL

58. THE GUILDHALL

59. THE MONUMENT

60. AT LONDON BRIDGE

61. ST. PAUL'S CATHEDRAL FROM SOUTHWARK

62. TOWER BRIDGE

63. VICTORIA AND ALBERT DOCK

64. THE TOWER OF LONDON FROM TOWER BRIDGE

65. GREENWICH OBSERVATORY AND THE MONUMENT TO GENERAL WOLFE

66A. ROYAL NAVAL COLLEGE, GREENWICH, FROM THE RIVER

66B. ROYAL NAVAL COLLEGE, GREENWICH: COLONNADE

67. ROYAL NAVAL COLLEGE, GREENWICH: THE CHAPEL

68A. QUEEN'S HOUSE AND ROYAL NAVAL COLLEGE, GREENWICH, FROM GREENWICH OBSERVATORY

68B. QUEEN'S HOUSE, GREENWICH

69. ROYAL NAVAL COLLEGE, GREENWICH: THE PAINTED HALL

70.   NO. 8 CLIFFORD STREET, MAYFAIR

71. ASHBURNHAM HOUSE, WESTMINSTER

72.   THEATRE ROYAL, HAYMARKET

73. MARBLE ARCH

74. AT THE SERPENTINE, KENSINGTON GARDENS

75. THE ALBERT MEMORIAL AND THE ROYAL ALBERT HALL

76. CONNAUGHT SQUARE

77. REGENT'S CANAL, PADDINGTON

78. MOTIF : REGENT'S CANAL, PADDINGTON

79.   VIEW FROM PRIMROSE HILL TOWARDS HAMPSTEAD

80.   HEATH STREET, HAMPSTEAD

81. GOLDEN YARD, HAMPSTEAD

82. HIGHGATE CEMETERY: THE CATACOMBS

83. HIGHGATE CEMETERY: ENTRANCE TO THE CATACOMBS

84. CHELSEA ROYAL HOSPITAL

85.   QUEEN ANNE'S GATE, WESTMINSTER

86. KEW GARDENS: THE PALM-HOUSE

87. KEW GARDENS: THE PAGODA

88.   HAMPTON COURT PALACE: BASE COURT

89. HAMPTON COURT PALACE: CLOCK COURT

90. HAMPTON COURT PALACE: THE KING'S GREAT STAIRCASE

91. HAMPTON COURT PALACE: FOUNTAIN COURT

92. HAMPTON COURT PALACE: CHAPEL ROYAL

93. HAMPTON COURT PALACE: CHAPEL ROYAL, DETAIL OF CEILING

94. CHISWICK PARK

95. CHISWICK PARK: THE BRIDGE

96. CHISWICK PARK: TEMPLE AND OBELISK

NOTES ON THE PLATES

BY HELMUT GERNSHEIM

ST. PAUL'S CATHEDRAL

St. Paul's Cathedral was built by Sir Christopher Wren between 1675 and 1710 on the site of Old St. Paul's, destroyed in the Fire of London, 1666. Unlike any other English cathedral, Wren's masterpiece is in Renaissance style, and is a homogeneous work, the inspiration of one architect and completed within his lifetime. St. Paul's is the fourth largest cathedral in the world, exceeded in size only by those of Rome, Seville, and Milan.

St. Paul's has been fittingly described as 'the parish church of the British Empire'. It is the scene of many State ceremonies, both of national rejoicing and national mourning, and ranks second only to Westminster Abbey as the last resting-place of the illustrious dead. When, towards the end of the eighteenth century, Westminster Abbey became overcrowded with monuments and no good sites worthy of national heroes could be found, a new Valhalla had to be created and the obvious choice was St. Paul's. The Dean and Chapter, who up to 1794 had 'preserved a Puritan tradition of iconophobia', suddenly reversed their policy and allowed sculptured monuments to be erected. Colossal sums were spent to commemorate fallen naval and military heroes in huge piles of stone. Apart from the Wellington monument, erected in 1852, the memorials in St. Paul's betray some of the worst excesses of monumental art, to which stands in poignant contrast the plain marble slab marking the grave of its architect, with its simple inscription, 'Lector, si monumentum requiris, circumspice'.

1. ST. PAUL'S CATHEDRAL FROM THE EAST

The imposing dome rising to 365 feet is the outstanding feature of London's skyline, but until the recent war the whole majestic structure of the cathedral was too closely hemmed in by houses to permit of a general view - a vista opened up by German bombs.

2. ST. PAUL'S CATHEDRAL: DECORATIVE SHELL WINDOW

The fine decorative carving on the exterior is small in scale and restrained in character, and thus is hardly visible at street level. A study of the many carved panels under the windows, and this little gem, will at once reveal that this stonework was executed with great skill by master-craftsmen (such as Grinling Gibbons and Francis Bird).

3. ST. PAUL'S CATHEDRAL: CAPITAL OF DRUM GALLERY, AND CLOCK TOWER

Cramming myself and the camera into a little niche where pigeons and starlings roost, I obtained a picture of superb detail from an angle from which few human eyes have seen it before.

4-5. ST. PAUL'S CATHEDRAL: SPIRAL STAIRCASE IN CLOCK TOWER, LOOKING UP AND LOOKING DOWN

Built in 1705, the splendid Geometrical Staircase, which runs inside the south-west tower to the triforium and to the Cathedral Library, was originally intended by Wren - so I have been told - to lead to an observatory which Charles II gave him permission to build in the tower, but Parliament withheld consent. The magnificence of the free-standing staircase is overpowering.

The regular 'snail' pattern of plate 4 was obtained by lying with the camera in the centre of the floor. The irregular pattern of plate 5 is due to the fact that it could not be photographed from the centre; the picture was taken from the balcony leading to the triforium.

6. ST. PAUL'S CATHEDRAL: LORD NELSON

Nelson seems to have hoped for burial at Westminster Abbey for it is reported that at the Battle of Cape St. Vincent he shouted, 'Westminster Abbey or glorious victory!' The huge monument in the south transept betrays little of Flaxman's usual neo-hellenism. Nelson stands on a pedestal adorned with allegorical figures, while Britannia points him out to two naval cadets.

7. ST. PAUL'S CATHEDRAL: UPPER GALLERY OF CLOCK TOWER

The west towers are perhaps St. Paul's most attractive features, for in them, as Dr. Margaret Whinney has pointed out, 'Wren exploits to a greater degree than anywhere else in his work those baroque qualities of a play of curve against curve,

113

of broken silhouettes, of ornaments designed to lead the eye from one stage to the next, and above all of motives arranged to give the maximum contrast of light and shade.' Externally the two towers are identical except for the clock in the south-west tower.

8. THE RUINS OF ST. MARY-LE-BOW

Bow church was perhaps the finest of the thirty City churches designed by Wren after the Fire of London. It was begun in 1671 and completed with the steeple in 1687. The church fell a victim to the Luftwaffe, except for the beautiful steeple. According to tradition only persons born within the sound of its famous peal of bells are Cockneys – true Londoners.

9. THE CHURCH OF ST. MARY-LE-STRAND

St. Mary-le-Strand was the first of fifty churches ordered during Queen Anne's reign to be built to replace those destroyed in the Great Fire. James Gibbs in his own account of St. Mary's, says it was the first building he was employed on after his ten years' studies in Italy. The finely proportioned church, built 1714-7, stands on an island site near Somerset House.

10. BURLINGTON HOUSE: THE ROYAL ACADEMY OF ARTS

The Royal Academy building was erected by Sydney Smirke in 1868-9 on the site of the town mansion of the Earls of Burlington, which had been demolished in 1867. The statues in the niches of the 'Renaissance' façade represent nine artists, from Phidias to Flaxman. The bronze statue in the courtyard is of Sir Joshua Reynolds, first President of the Royal Academy of Arts, founded in 1768.
The wings flanking the courtyard were built in 1872 and house several learned societies, including the Royal Society.

11. SOMERSET HOUSE

This palatial edifice dates from 1778 and was erected by Sir William Chambers on the site of the Duke of Somerset's palace. The east wing, occupied by King's College, was added by Sir Robert Smirke in 1829-34, and the west wing by Sir James Pennethorne in 1854. The building, now occupied by various public offices, originally housed the Royal Academy, Royal Society, and other learned societies now at Burlington House (plate 10). The bronze group in the courtyard represents George III with the British Lion and Father Thames at his feet. The imposing Palladian façade facing the river is 780 ft. long.
Canova is reported to have said that he would return to England from Italy at any time if only to look upon St. Paul's, Somerset House, and the interior of St. Stephen's, Walbrook – the latter unfortunately destroyed during the bombing.

12. THE ROYAL SOCIETY OF ARTS, JOHN ADAM STREET, ADELPHI

The Royal Society of Arts was established in 1754 for the encouragement of art, manufactures and commerce, and played a prominent part in promoting the International Exhibitions of 1851 and 1862. The façade (1772) in John Adam Street is a fine example of an Adam exterior.

13. OFFICES OF 'THE LANCET', ADAM STREET, ADELPHI

A stone's throw from the Royal Society of Arts is another exquisite example of architecture with all the charm and delicacy of an Adam frontage. The four Scottish brothers Robert, John, James and William Adam created what is known as the Adam style, not only in architecture but also in interior decoration and furniture. In 1768 they obtained a 99 years' lease of the district which is called after the brothers, 'The Adelphi'.

14. TRAFALGAR SQUARE: VIEW TOWARDS WESTMINSTER

Trafalgar Square, named in commemoration of Nelson's great victory, is the finest and largest square in London and a favourite rendezvous for political demonstrations, the orators speaking from the plinth of Nelson's column, which rises to a height of 193 feet and is surmounted by a statue of the hero. It was erected in 1849 from a design by William Railton.

15. TRAFALGAR SQUARE AND ST. MARTIN'S-IN-THE-FIELDS

On three sides Trafalgar Square is bounded by stately buildings: to the west lie Canada House and the Royal College of Physicians, to the north the National Gallery, and to the east St. Martin's-in-the-Fields and South Africa House.
St. Martin's-in-the-Fields was erected 1721-6 by James Gibbs, a pupil of Sir Christopher Wren. The exterior of the church has remained practically unaltered from Gibbs's day up to the present. The fine steeple and the elegant portico in the Greek style are seen to the best advantage from Trafalgar Square.
Four colossal bronze lions designed by Sir Edwin Landseer guard the base of Nelson's column.

16. THE NATIONAL GALLERY AND ST. MARTIN'S-IN-THE-FIELDS

London affords few fine street views, but the approach to Trafalgar Square from Pall Mall is one of the best. The portico on the right is the entrance to the Royal College of Physicians, built by Sir Robert Smirke (1825).

17. TRAFALGAR SQUARE AND THE NATIONAL GALLERY

The National Gallery stands in a commanding position on a terrace on the north side of Trafalgar Square. The centre block was erected in 1832-8 from designs by W. Wilkins, and there have been considerable extensions at various times to accommodate the ever-growing collection, today regarded as one of the finest in the world.

18. WATERLOO PLACE

Undoubtedly the finest vista in London is obtained from the foot of the Duke of York's Column looking towards Piccadilly Circus. The view is unspoilt by mean commercialism, large hoardings, or bad Victorian architecture, which so often obtrude unpleasantly upon an otherwise pleasant scene. To the right and left of the Edward VII Memorial lies aristocratic clubland. On the left is the Athenaeum Club (plate 19), on the right the United Service Club, in a house built by John Nash in 1828.

The two horse-mounting blocks at the kerb were put there at the request of the Duke of Wellington in 1830.

19. THE ATHENAEUM CLUB

The leading literary and learned club, founded in 1824, occupies a stately building erected in 1830 by Decimus Burton. The portico is surmounted by a statue of Athena; the frieze is supposed to be a reproduction of that of the Parthenon, executed by John Henning in the same size as the original. The rather disturbing plain top storey was added in 1900 to provide a smoking-room.

20. ST. JAMES'S PALACE: THE GATEHOUSE

The picturesque sixteenth-century gatehouse with its four octagonal towers, facing St. James's Street, is one of the few remaining parts of the palace which Henry VII had built here, and which was destroyed by fire in 1809. Many sovereigns lived here from time to time, the last being William IV, who made it his principal residence. Until the death of the Prince Consort in 1861, Queen Victoria held her levées and drawing rooms at St. James's Palace. It is still used occasionally for royal functions, and foreign ambassadors traditionally present their credentials to the Court of St. James's, although this function now takes place at Buckingham Palace.

The more recent wings of the Palace are let to deserving servants of the Crown and their dependants as a mark of special favour.

21. ST. JAMES'S SQUARE, WITH THE STATUE OF WILLIAM III

One of the earliest squares to be laid out in the West End (in the reign of Charles II), St. James's Square continued to be an aristocratic place of residence until after the first world war. No. 10, now occupied by the Royal Institute of International Affairs, is noteworthy as having been the abode of three Prime Ministers – William Pitt the Elder, Lord Derby, and Mr. Gladstone. Though the houses surrounding the square are now largely occupied by clubs and organizations such as the Arts Council of Great Britain and the London Library, it has retained its atmosphere of elegance better than any other London square.

The bronze equestrian statue of William III is by John Bacon (1808).

22. BOODLE'S CLUB, ST. JAMES'S STREET

Among the many clubs in St. James's Street, Boodle's, Brooks's and White's are among the oldest and most famous. During the eighteenth century they were distinguished for fashion and gambling. Boodle's at No. 28, founded in 1762, has the finest edifice – by Adam (compare with plate 12).

23. BROOKS'S CLUB, ST. JAMES'S STREET

Brooks's Club at No. 60 St. James's Street was founded in 1764. It was the leading Whig club, and the rival of White's, the principal Tory club. William Pitt the Younger, Charles James Fox and Sheridan were all members of Brooks's. The club premises were built by Henry Holland in 1777-8. The photograph shows the charming staircase-well, with a bust of William Pitt.

24. ST. GEORGE'S CHURCH, HANOVER SQUARE

In George Street, which runs south from Hanover Square, stands St. George's church, with an elegant Corinthian portico, built in 1713-24 by James, a pupil of James Gibbs. It is particularly famous for fashionable weddings. Among the notable people married here were Sir William Hamilton and Nelson's Emma, 1791; Disraeli in 1839; Lola Montez in 1849; George Eliot in 1880; Theodore Roosevelt in 1886; Lord Oxford and Asquith in 1894.

25. THE GROSVENOR CHAPEL, SOUTH AUDLEY STREET

Walking down Park Lane from Grosvenor House to Dorchester House, one catches a glimpse of this simple little eighteenth-century chapel (1730), a picturesque bit of London which survived the bombing. Here the American forces held divine service during the 1939-45 war.

26. THE WELLINGTON ARCH, GREEN PARK

Designed by Decimus Burton in 1828, the arch originally stood opposite the main entrance to Hyde Park, whence it was transferred to its present position at the west end of Green Park in 1883. The bronze group representing Peace in her quadriga was added by Adrian Jones in 1912. The arch takes its name from a hideous and colossal equestrian statue of the victor of Waterloo, for many years the butt of Londoners, which surmounted the arch until it was banished to Aldershot.

27. CARLTON HOUSE TERRACE, THE MALL

The leading exponent of the Regency style was John Nash, the town planner of the Prince Regent (later George IV). Of Nash it was said –
'Augustus at Rome was for building renown'd,
For of marble he left what of brick he had found;
But is not our Nash, too, a very great master,
He finds us all brick and he leaves us all plaster?'
The fine terraces of stuccoed houses round Regent's Park, and Carlton House Terrace on the north side of St. James's Park, are his most perfect creations. Nash was not so much concerned with ornamentation as with broad architectural effects. At one time Carlton House Terrace was mainly occupied by the aristocracy, but now the houses serve as clubs and government offices.

28. PICCADILLY CIRCUS

The most famous traffic centre in the West End, both above and below ground, is Piccadilly Circus. 775,000 passengers a week use the Underground station; 42,000 vehicles pass every day between 8 am. and 8 p.m.
Its central position in the heart of the theatre, restaurant, and shopping district make Piccadilly Circus the meeting place of friends, and the rendezvous of lovers from the late afternoon until the early morning hours. The graceful winged archer by Alfred Gilbert on the memorial to the Earl of Shaftesbury has, quite understandably, been unofficially christened 'Eros'.

29. ROYAL HORSE GUARD, WHITEHALL

Another focal point of popular attraction is the Horse Guards, Whitehall, where the picturesque ceremony of mounting the Guard takes place every weekday morning at eleven o'clock (Sundays at 10 a.m.); at 4 p.m. the Guard is dismounted. The two mounted sentinels of the Household Cavalry at the gate are relieved every hour.

30. RELIEVING THE GUARD, BUCKINGHAM PALACE

The Guards in their scarlet coats and bearskins, posted outside Buckingham Palace, St. James's Palace and Marlborough House, are relieved every two hours. The traditional pageantry of Changing the Guard usually takes place every other day, sometimes at Buckingham Palace, at other times at St. James's Palace, depending on the season and whether or not the Queen is in residence.

31. NO. 10, DOWNING STREET

No. 10, Downing Street was built about 1663 by Sir George Downing. It has been the official residence of the Prime Minister since 1735, and is the usual scene of Cabinet meetings. The simple façade is famous out of all proportion to its appearance. Actually No. 10 is much more commodious than its narrow, dingy, brick exterior suggests, for it incorporates two houses; the second house, built by Sir Christopher Wren c. 1677, faces the Horse Guards' Parade and contains the famous Cabinet Room.

32. BUCKINGHAM PALACE AND THE QUEEN VICTORIA MEMORIAL

Buckingham Palace is situated at the west end of St. James's Park, occupying the site and deriving its name from the town mansion of the Duke of Buckingham, which was purchased by George III. Buckingham Palace was begun in the reign of George IV from the designs of John Nash (1825) but was not used as a royal residence until Queen Victoria's accession. Since then it has been extended and altered out of recognition. The simple and dignified façade facing St. James's Park was only added in 1913.
The over-elaborate and unattractive memorial to Queen Victoria in front of the Palace was erected in 1911.

33. THE ADMIRALTY, WHITEHALL

One of the most attractive of the government offices in Whitehall is the Old Admiralty. Built by Thomas Ripley 1724-6, its tall classical portico and small courtyard are masked from Whitehall by an elegant stone screen designed by the brothers Adam in 1760.

34. ST. JAMES'S PARK: VIEW TOWARDS WHITEHALL

The present appearance of St. James's Park was imparted to it by John Nash in 1827-9. The beautiful clumps of trees, the winding lake, and the charming views of Buckingham Palace and Whitehall, combine to make it the most attractive of the London parks. The suspension bridge over the lake commands a famous view of Whitehall, the cupolas and towers of the new Admiralty building having a surprisingly Oriental look from this distance.

35. LANCASTER HOUSE, GREEN PARK

Long known as Stafford House after its owner, the Marquis of Stafford, later Duke of Sutherland, this mansion enjoyed the reputation of being the most sumptuous private residence in London. As is often the case in this country, the simple term 'House' denotes what would be called a palace in any other land. Stafford House was built by

Benjamin Wyatt c. 1825; the top storey is a later addition by Sir Charles Barry, who also designed the grand staircase. In 1912 Lord Leverhulme purchased the mansion and presented it to the nation for the purpose of housing the London Museum. In recent years Lancaster House has provided the setting for several international conferences; the Conference of Foreign Ministers in May 1950 was held there.

36. HORSE GUARDS, WHITEHALL

The charming building with a clock-tower almost opposite James I's Banqueting Hall was erected in 1751-3 from designs by William Kent. The forecourt is the scene of the colourful military ceremony referred to in plate 29. A passage beneath the clock-tower leads to the Horse Guards' Parade, a very large quadrangle where the imposing pageantry of Trooping the Colour is annually performed by the Guards on the King's official birthday, June 3rd.

37. BIG BEN AND THE HOUSES OF PARLIAMENT

The Houses of Parliament, or Palace of Westminster, as this stately neo-Gothic edifice is sometimes called, extends for an unbroken length of 940 feet along the Thames. Though the architectural style may not be to everyone's taste, there can be no doubt that it is an imposing sight with its towers, pinnacles and turrets. It was erected 1840-50 from designs by Sir Charles Barry, the old Houses having been burned down in 1834. St. Stephen's Tower houses the bell known all over the world as Big Ben.

38. THE HOUSES OF PARLIAMENT, FROM THE ROOF OF HENRY VII's CHAPEL, WESTMINSTER ABBEY

To look across the roof of Henry VII's Chapel towards the central spire of the Houses of Parliament affords an interesting comparison between genuine and Victorian Gothic.

39. WESTMINSTER ABBEY: HENRY VII's CHAPEL

Built in 1503-19, this chapel is the finest example of the late Perpendicular style. The superb fan-vaulting is of unrivalled beauty. The profuse decoration of statues along the walls, the splendid tomb of its founder, the picturesque banners of the Knights of the Bath, the elaborate carving of the stalls, all give an overpowering effect of magnificence.
Originally begun as a shrine for Henry VI (who, however, still rests at Windsor), the chapel was continued as a mausoleum for its founder, Henry VII. Here is the magnificent Renaissance tomb, surrounded by a big iron grille, by the Florentine artist Pietro Torrigiano, with bronze effigies of Henry VII and his wife. The side aisles and side chapels contain the tombs of many kings and queens. Others are in Edward the Confessor's Chapel, but by no means all the kings and queens of England are buried in Westminster Abbey, and of those who are, only comparatively few are commemorated by effigies. The earliest effigies are those of Henry III and his daughter-in-law, Eleanor of Castile, the first wife of Edward I. There are also effigies of the following kings and queens: Edward III and Philippa of Hainault, Richard II and his first wife, Anne of Bohemia, the headless oak figure of Henry V (the silver head was stolen and melted down in Henry VIII's reign), Henry VII and Elizabeth of York, Mary, Queen of Scots, and Queen Elizabeth.

40. WESTMINSTER ABBEY: HENRY III, (REIGNED 1227-72)

In Edward the Confessor's Chapel is the earliest royal effigy in the Abbey. It is the work of William Torel, a London goldsmith (1291-2) and is of gilded bronze. The king's crown, ornamented with trefoils, was formerly adorned with artificial jewels.

41. WESTMINSTER ABBEY: EDWARD III, (REIGNED 1327-77)

The gilded bronze effigy in Edward the Confessor's Chapel is probably by John Orchard. The saint-like face cannot be considered to be a portrait; it is an idealized representation, rather unsuitable for a soldier king. Originally a crown was set upon the king's head, and the mark where it rested is clearly visible.

42-3. WESTMINSTER ABBEY: HENRY VII, (REIGNED 1485-1509)

This gilded bronze effigy is by Pietro Torrigiani. It is clearly a portrait of the king, who wears a flat-topped cap with lappets. His head rests on a cushion; his beautifully modelled hands are folded in prayer.

44. WESTMINSTER ABBEY: STAG AT THE FEET OF LADY MARGARET BEAUFORT, MOTHER OF HENRY VII

The bronze effigy of Lady Margaret Beaufort in Henry VII's Chapel was also executed by Torrigiani. It was his first commission in England (1511) and is regarded by many as his masterpiece.

45. WESTMINSTER ABBEY: CHERUB FROM TOMB OF HENRY VII

The gilded bronze cherub is one of four sitting on the corners of the tomb of Henry VII and Elizabeth of York. They, too, are from the hand of Torrigiano. The cherubs, like the royal effigies, were photographed at their place of evacuation during the war and for this reason are not shown *in situ.*

MONUMENTS IN WESTMINSTER ABBEY

Westminster Abbey has been called the British Valhalla in the nineteenth century, and the National Shrine in the twentieth. The historic associations which are so closely woven into its fabric draw to the Abbey every year thousands of visitors who wander around aimlessly, lost in the spaciousness and gloom of the interior and bewildered by the profusion of monuments to famous and insignificant people alike. For though the Abbey is the last resting-place of many who were great in their achievements, the memory of many other great men is perpetuated by a monument or epitaph only and they are buried elsewhere. There are also a great many monuments to insignificant people, for up to the end of the 'seventies of the last century, the erection of a monument in the Abbey depended on the right of birth or on payment of a large fee to the Dean and Chapter, and 'the best sites were reserved for those who could pay best for them, while a nook was all that could be conceded to men of imperishable fame.' The power of helping obscure friends to fame by purchase prevailed to a large degree, and in comparison with the sumptuous monuments to the memory of unknown persons, those erected in memory of the great English poets sometimes appear mean. Addison caustically commented on this in *The Spectator:* 'In the poetical quarter I found there were poets who had no monuments, and monuments which had no poets.' Byron was denied a place in the Abbey on moral grounds, and neither Keats nor Shelley has so far been commemorated by as much as a tablet. On the other hand, the only qualification which procured a monument to one John Phillips seems to have been a poem on the qualities of cider, and a certain Thomas Smith is only remembered for the curious inscription on the tablet: 'Who through ye spotted vaile of the smallpox rendered a pure and unspotted soul to God.'

46-7. WESTMINSTER ABBEY: SIR ISAAC NEWTON, D. 1727

After the Royal effigies, the Newton monument is probably the most important in the Abbey. It was erected four years after the great scientist's death, in the most prominent position in the nave.
The monument was designed by William Kent and sculptured by John Michael Rysbrack, who came from Antwerp, settled in England, and became one of the most famous sculptors of his day. Newton leans on the four folios which brought him fame: *Divinity, Chronology, Optics* and *Philo-*

sophiae Naturalis Principia Mathematica. His left hand points to two cherubs reciting his achievements from a scroll. Above the group is the celestial globe with the constellations, and reclining on it an allegorical figure representing Astronomy. Sir Kenneth Clark called this head 'a masterpiece of baroque portraiture, heroic, yet eloquent and human.'

48. WESTMINSTER ABBEY: DR. JOHNSON, D. 1784

This portrait in stone of the famous lexicographer is by Nollekens. The front view of the bust is not particularly attractive because of the Doctor's fat, flabby face. The profile is certainly more flattering, and the play of light and shade gives a lifelike appearance to the bust.

49. WESTMINSTER ABBEY: HANDEL, D. 1759

The monument to the great composer was erected in 1762 and is by Roubiliac, who made his name in London with another statue of Handel for Vauxhall Gardens in 1738. Roubiliac, who originally came from France, is one of the three great baroque sculptors who worked in England. He knew Handel well and we can assume that the life-size figure is a good likeness. We imagine Handel here as the bustling director of one of his operas rather than as the composer of the great oratorio 'The Messiah', from which a few bars of the famous aria 'I know that my Redeemer liveth' are recorded on the marble music sheet.

50. WESTMINSTER ABBEY: THE LITTLE CLOISTERS

A dark vaulted passage from the Cloisters to Westminster School branches off to the left and leads to the charming Little Cloisters. Around the courtyard are the dwellings of several Abbey dignitaries, though several of the houses were burned down during one of the air-raids in the last war.

51. WESTMINSTER ABBEY: THE CLOISTERS

The present Cloisters were begun in the thirteenth century and completed, except for a very small part, by 1366. They have unfortunately been much spoiled by restoration at various times. Much of the window-tracery in the north Cloisters shown here was renewed by Sir Giles Gilbert Scott towards the end of the last century.

52. THREE THAMES BRIDGES

Much of the beauty of the river flowing through eighteenth-century London, so incomparably portrayed by Canaletto, has, unfortunately been lost with the growth of London as a port and its increased industrialization. But the river still offers some fine views, and has often been glorified by famous artists. To Gustave Doré it offered as subjects people at work and at play on the river; Whistler and Monet were inspired chiefly by its astonishing atmospheric effects.

53. THE EMBANKMENT

One of the best river views that can still be enjoyed is from the Embankment on the south side, outside St. Thomas's Hospital. Here we see Big Ben on the left, and beyond Westminster Bridge, Shell-Mex House and the City.

54A. GATE OF ST. BARTHOLOMEW THE GREAT

The church of St. Bartholomew, Smithfield, is approached through a picturesque Elizabethan half-timbered gateway, accidentally brought to light in 1915 by a German bomb which loosened the plaster concealing it (see also plate 56).

54B. THE OLD CURIOSITY SHOP

In a little side street off Kingsway stands the Old Curiosity Shop, established in 1567, and associated in many people's minds with Little Nell and her grandfather in Charles Dickens's 'Old Curiosity Shop' (1840).

55. THE GEORGE INN, SOUTHWARK

South of London Bridge in the district of Southwark stands this old coaching inn, once a great terminus for the south-east of England. It is the last galleried inn left in London, and was built in 1676. The outside galleries with their heavy balustrades form the only passage-way from one room to another. The inn is mentioned by Dickens in 'Little Dorrit'.

56. ST. BARTHOLOMEW THE GREAT, SMITHFIELD

Founded in 1123 by Rahere, a minstrel and favourite of Henry I, St. Bartholomew is the oldest parish church in London. Of the original Augustinian Priory Church there remains only the choir, transept, and one bay of the nave which was added before 1170. The massive columns, piers and round arches, are in pure Norman style. The clerestory, however, above the Norman triforium, is Perpendicular, having been rebuilt early in the fifteenth century. On the north side of the choir is the early fifteenth-century tomb of the founder (died 1143) beneath a richly decorated canopy. In the triforium opposite is a beautiful late Perpendicular oriel, added by Prior Bolton, whose rebus, a bolt through a tun, it bears.

57. GATE OF ST. BARTHOLOMEW'S HOSPITAL

The hospital originally formed part of the Augustinian Priory of St. Bartholomew, and like it, was founded by Rahere, in fulfilment of a vow made by him while lying ill in Rome. It is the oldest institution of the kind in England. The Hospital, which is situated at the south-east side of Smithfield market, was enlarged several times. The main entrance is through an imposing gateway erected in 1702–4 by Edward Strong; it is a masterpiece known to few people. The statue of Henry VIII was put there in gratitude for his having spared the Hospital at the Dissolution of the Monasteries in 1546, when the Priory was almost completely demolished. The two other figures represent Lameness and Sickness.

58. THE GUILDHALL

The Guildhall, situated at the end of King Street, Cheapside, was built 1411–35 on the site of an earlier structure. Most of the medieval timber-work was destroyed by the Great Fire in 1666. A complete restoration was undertaken in 1789 by the City Architect, George Dance the Younger, and the 'Gothic' façade dates from this period. It survived the last war, in which again much damage was caused to other parts of the building.

59. THE MONUMENT

Between Billingsgate fish-market and London Bridge, rises The Monument, a Doric column 202 feet high. It was erected from the designs of Sir Christopher Wren in 1671–7, to commemorate the Great Fire of London, which broke out on September 2nd 1666 in Pudding Lane at a point supposed to be exactly 202 feet from The Monument. The fire, which lasted for six days, destroyed 460 streets, with 89 churches and 13,200 houses. There is an interesting view from the platform, which can be reached by a winding staircase inside the column.

60. AT LONDON BRIDGE

The hustle and bustle of loading and unloading ocean-going ships in the heart of London has a fascination of its own. Owing to the tide, and the twin drawbridges of Tower Bridge (plate 62), large ships can come up the Thames as far as London Bridge.

61. ST. PAUL'S CATHEDRAL, FROM SOUTHWARK

Though the south bank of the river is mostly closed in with wharves and warehouses, it is worth exploring east of Blackfriars Bridge, for little passages like the one depicted lead right to the river and open up surprising views.

62. TOWER BRIDGE

Tower Bridge, the 'gateway of the City', was opened in 1894. It is novel in design, having twin drawbridges between the abutment towers, to allow for the passage of large vessels. A warning bell is rung when the two bascules are about to be raised, which only takes a minute and a half, so there is very little interference with the great stream of traffic which constantly flows across the bridge. Ships pass under the bridge only at high tide. It is a sight well worth watching from the pleasant gun wharf just outside the Tower of London.

63. VICTORIA & ALBERT DOCKS

The long chain of docks extending from Tower Bridge to Tilbury handles one-third of the imports and a quarter of the exports of the United Kingdom. 'The miles of quays, the colossal warehouses, the vast basins filled with shipping of every description, provide a sight calculated to stir the blood of the most phlegmatic of Englishmen, and to excite the envy of "our friend the foreigner" '. The largest and most modern docks, which can be reached by train from Fenchurch Street station, are the Royal Victoria & Albert Docks, opened in 1885, and the King George V Dock, opened in 1921, which can accommodate the largest liners and battleships afloat.

64. THE TOWER OF LONDON FROM TOWER BRIDGE

This irregular mass of buildings surrounded by a battlemented wall and a deep moat (drained in 1843) is historically the most important building in England. It has served the three purposes of a fortress, a royal residence, and a state prison. The great central keep with four turrets, prominent in this photograph, is known as the White Tower. It is the most ancient part, begun in 1078 by William the Conqueror. Visitors to the Tower can see the Crown Jewels, a famous collection of armour, and the prisons and place of execution of many people famous in history.

65. GREENWICH OBSERVATORY, AND THE MONUMENT TO GENERAL WOLFE

Founded in 1675 by Charles II 'for the purpose of ascertaining the motions of the moon, and the places of the fixed stars, as a means of discovering that great desideratum, the longitude at sea', the Royal Observatory stands on a hill in Greenwich Park. The main body of the unpretentious building is by Sir Christopher Wren. The zero meridian of longitude is reckoned from this spot, and the correct time for the whole of England is set by the Observatory.

The terrace in front of the Observatory commands a fine view over Queen's House and the palatial buildings of the Royal Naval College (plate 68A) and beyond the river, over Hainault and Epping Forests, to the heights of Hampstead.

66A. ROYAL NAVAL COLLEGE, GREENWICH, FROM THE RIVER

The finest approach to Greenwich is by water-bus from Westminster Bridge or Tower Bridge - passing between the ships of all nations, with huge warehouses, quays and wharves on either side - for the imposing Palace of Greenwich, now the home of the Royal Naval College, is seen to best advantage from the river.

Only the crypt remains of the Royal Palace, which was begun here in 1433, and afterwards became the favourite residence of the Tudor sovereigns. Here Henry VIII and his daughters Queen Mary and Queen Elizabeth were born, and here his son Edward VI died. During the Commonwealth the Palace fell into decay and Charles II began a new building, of which, however, only the west wing by John Webb was erected. Under William and Mary the east wing and the domed buildings were added in 1705 from designs by Sir Christopher Wren, and the whole palace was converted into a home for old and disabled seamen. Successive sovereigns added new buildings and 'Greenwich Hospital' was only completed by George II. In 1873 it was assigned to the Royal Naval College for the education of naval officers.

66B. ROYAL NAVAL COLLEGE, GREENWICH: THE COLONNADE

On the west side of the elegant stone colonnade is a bas-relief in the pediment by Benjamin West, depicting the victories and death of Nelson.

67. ROYAL NAVAL COLLEGE, GREENWICH: THE CHAPEL

The exterior is identical with that of the Painted Hall opposite. Both were built by Sir Christopher Wren, but the interior of the chapel was destroyed by fire in 1779. The redecoration, which was started almost at once, was entrusted to James ('Athenian') Stuart, and exhibits an abundance of classical stucco ornamentation, of which a fine example is reproduced on p. 7.

68A. QUEEN'S HOUSE AND ROYAL NAVAL COLLEGE, GREENWICH, FROM GREENWICH OBSERVATORY

See plate 65, second paragraph.

68B. QUEEN'S HOUSE, GREENWICH

This beautiful villa, originally designed by Inigo Jones in 1617 for Anne of Denmark, was finished in 1635 for Henrietta Maria. Inigo Jones, who had studied in Italy, introduced the Palladian style of architecture into England with this house, which is regarded as his masterpiece. It now houses the Royal Maritime Museum.

69. ROYAL NAVAL COLLEGE, GREENWICH: THE PAINTED HALL

The Painted Hall, which serves as dining hall for the Royal Naval College, takes its name from the ceiling painted by Sir James Thornhill, the great baroque painter, in 1708-1727. Allegorical paintings surround William and Mary in the Great Hall, and Queen Anne and her consort in the Upper Hall. The Hall is 106 feet long, 50 feet wide and 50 feet high, and is considered one of the grandest in Britain.

70. NO. 8, CLIFFORD STREET, MAYFAIR

This fine town house, once the property of Admiral Sir Edward Harvey, was built between 1720 and 1730. The allegorical paintings which adorn the walls of the staircase-well and illustrate the story of Diana and Endymion, and other legends, were probably executed by Sir James Thornhill. The photograph illustrates Pallas Athene within a painted niche at the head of the staircase - an ingenious use of a 'sculptural' motif in painting.

71. ASHBURNHAM HOUSE, WESTMINSTER

Ashburnham House was built about 1660 by John Webb, a nephew of Inigo Jones. Its unpretentious red brick exterior hides a stately interior. The superb staircase, with its fine panelling and fluted columns, which may be based on a design of Inigo Jones, is a masterpiece, of which Mr. Sacheverell Sitwell wrote, 'It would be no exaggeration, remembering the staircases in Italian palaces, to say that this, within its modest dimensions, is as fine as any.'

The house is named after Colonel William Ashburnham, a noted Royalist and personal friend of Charles II, who occupied it in 1662. In 1882 it was incorporated in the Westminster School buildings.

72. THEATRE ROYAL, HAYMARKET

The present building by John Nash, 1820-21, stands on the site of an earlier theatre by Vanburgh. In interior decoration it is perhaps the finest theatre in London.

73. MARBLE ARCH

Marble Arch takes its name from the Carrara marble from which it is made. It was designed by John Nash more or less in the style of the triumphal arch of Constantine, and embellished with sculpture by Flaxman, Westmacott and Rossi. It was intended by George IV to form the portal of Buckingham Palace and was erected there in 1828. By a miscalculation the centre arch was too narrow to admit the State Coach. On completion of the new east wing in 1850 the arch was removed from the Palace and in the following year it was erected in its present position. Originally it was intended that the equestrian statue of George IV by Chantrey - now in Trafalgar Square - should surmount the arch. The proposed function of the arch as a special entrance for the sovereign and royal family has been maintained, and the centre gate is opened only for them.

74. AT THE SERPENTINE, KENSINGTON GARDENS

Kensington Gardens and Hyde Park, which adjoin one another, together form the largest open space in Central London. Through them winds the Serpentine, an artificial lake formed at the instigation of Queen Caroline, wife of George II, who had a string of existing ponds enlarged into one lake, which stretches from Lancaster Gate to the dell not far from Hyde Park Corner. At the Bayswater end stands a charming pavilion, and a stone basin flanked by two female figures, lending the whole a delightfully Italianate atmosphere.

75. THE ALBERT MEMORIAL AND THE ROYAL ALBERT HALL

At the south side of Kensington Gardens, not far from the site of the Great Exhibition of 1851, in the arrangement of which Prince Albert was largely instrumental, rises the Albert Memorial, which Queen Victoria and the nation erected in 1872. The monument, designed by Sir George Gilbert Scott, is a typical piece of Victoriana in its over-elaboration and profusion of bronze and marble statues, gilding, coloured stones and mosaics, all in atrocious taste. Prince Albert sits aloft, still turning the pages of the exhibition catalogue.

The Royal Albert Hall of Arts and Sciences, a vast amphitheatre, was erected partly with surplus money from the 1851 Exhibition and was constructed in 1867-71 by Captains Fowke and Scott. It is the largest hall in Europe and can accommodate 10,000 people. Originally designed for concerts, scientific and art assemblies, it is now also used for religious and political mass meetings, boxing matches, and charity balls. The organ is one of the largest in the world. The acoustics of the hall are notoriously bad.

76. CONNAUGHT SQUARE

This is just a typical London square. The quiet residential squares are a feature of London town planning, and those west of Edgware Road have so far escaped the fate of the more fashionable squares, which have been invaded by blocks of flats and offices.

77-8. REGENT'S CANAL, PADDINGTON.

Regent's Canal, exclusively used for barge traffic, runs from the dock area north to Victoria Park, then turns west, traverses the north side of Regent's Park and unites with the Paddington Canal, which forms part of the continuous waterway to Liverpool known as the Grand Union Canal. The section of the canal by Blomfield Road, Paddington, gives the district quite a Dutch appearance.

79. VIEW FROM PRIMROSE HILL TOWARDS HAMPSTEAD

Few visitors to London – indeed, few Londoners – would believe that within two miles of Oxford Circus one can find such a 'Constable' view. It was taken from my studio, and the spire in the distance is that of Christ Church, Hampstead.

80. HEATH STREET, HAMPSTEAD

81. GOLDEN YARD, HAMPSTEAD

Hampstead, and particularly the old village, is well worth a visit. The highest parts of the Heath command extensive views over London and the surrounding country. Old Hampstead, with its picturesque eighteenth-century and Regency houses, hilly streets, quaintly irregular courts and alleys, amply repays exploration. Here lived Constable, some of whose most famous pictures were inspired by the locality; Keats lived in Well Walk and later at Lawn Bank (now the Keats Museum); Romney's timber house still stands, at the top of Holly Bush Hill; not far from it is George Du Maurier's house, and the 'Admiral's House' – the abode of Sir Giles Gilbert Scott. Dr. Johnson stayed in Hampstead village for a time, and the famous Kit-Cat Club, which numbered among its members Congreve, Kneller, Addison, Steele and Pope, held its first meetings at a tavern in Hampstead. On the way from the pond, where Shelley is said to have sailed paper boats for children, to the stately eighteenth-century mansion of Ken Wood, stands the Spaniard's Inn, the gathering point of the 'No Popery' rioters of 1780, described by Dickens in 'Barnaby Rudge'.

82-3. HIGHGATE CEMETERY: THE CATACOMBS

Like Hampstead, Highgate is situated on a hill overlooking Hampstead Heath. Here are a number of elegant eighteenth-century residences; particularly noteworthy is 'The Grove', where Coleridge lived at No. 3. On the slope of the hill just below St. Michael's church (1833) is Highgate Cemetery, the grounds of which were laid out in about 1838. Two curious features, known to few people, are the 'Egyptian' avenue and the catacombs – the only ones in Britain. The entrance to the avenue (plate 83), flanked by two pairs of 'Egyptian' double columns and obelisks, and overshadowed by a drooping poplar tree, is one of the most striking bits of landscape gardening in London. On each side of the avenue are sepulchres furnished with stone shelves for the coffins. The avenue terminates in a sunken circular road (plate 82), flanked by similar sepulchres. The inner circle thus forms a large 'building' with a flat roof, from the middle of which rises a beautiful

cedar of Lebanon. The whole resembles a miniature city of tombs in the Egyptian style of architecture, to which the neo-gothic church of St. Michael on the summit of the hill forms a curious contrast in the background.

Among the many famous people buried in Highgate Cemetery are Karl Marx, Michael Faraday, J. M. W. Turner and George Eliot.

84. CHELSEA ROYAL HOSPITAL

Magnificently situated on the north bank of the Thames in a fine residential district full of literary and artistic associations stands this famous institution for old and disabled soldiers, founded by Charles II and built by Sir Christopher Wren in 1682-92. The building consists of a centre block and two wings. In the middle of the quadrangle stands a bronze statue of Charles II by Grinling Gibbons. On the left of the photograph can be seen specimens of the mortar shells used in 1855 in the Crimean War. The gun was captured in the Sikh War, 1849.

85. QUEEN ANNE'S GATE, WESTMINSTER

Queen Anne's Gate, on the south side of St. James's Park, is the most perfect example in London of the domestic architecture of the Queen Anne period. This quiet and unspoilt street was built by William Paterson. In front of No. 13 stands an old statue of the last of the Stuart sovereigns.

86. KEW GARDENS: THE PALM-HOUSE

87. KEW GARDENS: THE PAGODA

A visit to the Royal Botanic Gardens at Kew, the finest and most famous in the world, is a favourite outing for Londoners. Apart from the glasshouses, the museums and the herbarium, there are extensive informal grounds, with a lake and patches of woodland – a delightful spot for picnics. The real founder of Kew Gardens was the Princess of Wales, mother of George III, who began the formation of an exotic garden in 1759-60. The Chinese pagoda (plate 87) and the small Greek temples were designed for her by Sir William Chambers in 1760-62. In the northern part of the grounds is the modest seventeenth-century 'Dutch House' called Kew Palace, for it was used as a residence by George IV when Prince of Wales, and by George III during his attacks of insanity.

The Gardens were thrown open to the public in 1841 and soon afterwards (1844-8) the 362 ft. long Palm-house (plate 86) was erected by Decimus Burton.

HAMPTON COURT PALACE

What Versailles is to Paris, Hampton Court Palace is to London. The delightful excursion, by train from Waterloo station or, better still, by boat up the Thames from Richmond, should not be missed by any visitor to London.

The beautiful and stately edifice, the largest and finest of all the royal palaces in Britain, was begun by Cardinal Wolsey in 1515, with the intention of making it the most magnificent residence in England. Thirteen years later he 'presented' his mansion to Henry VIII in a vain attempt to regain his favour. The king at once began to enlarge it, adding the Great Hall.

Though the Tudor Palace was spacious enough, it did not suit the taste of William and Mary, who commissioned Sir Christopher Wren to plan a new building. He made extensive alterations, adding the east and south wings (1689–1718), which are the finest example of the Louis XIV style in England, yet without the pomposity of the Sun King's gorgeous palace. Wren was also responsible for laying out the gardens in the formal French style of the period.

Hampton Court Palace was a favourite residence of the sovereigns from Henry VIII to George II. George III and IV preferred Kew. Queen Victoria threw open to the public the gardens, the State Apartments and the orangery containing the famous Mantegna cartoons 'The Triumph of Julius Caesar' – the gem of the Royal art collections. The Palace contains in addition about a thousand rooms, of which about eight hundred have been converted into flats and granted 'by grace and favour' of the sovereign to the dependants of distinguished servants of the Crown.

88. HAMPTON COURT PALACE: BASE COURT

The Base Court, the first and largest of the three principal courts, was built by Cardinal Wolsey. Surrounding it are the lodgings in which his retinue or his guests were housed. The photograph shows the second gate tower known as Anne Boleyn's gateway. The bell turret above is an eighteenth-century addition; the clock was brought here from St. James's Palace by William IV. Over the arch are carved the royal arms of Henry VIII, and the terracotta medallions at the sides are by Giovanni da Maiano and were presented to Cardinal Wolsey by Pope Leo X.

89. HAMPTON COURT PALACE: CLOCK COURT

The Clock Court takes its name from the ingenious astronomical clock above the entrance, made for Henry VIII in 1540 and still working. This was the main courtyard of Wolsey's manor, but has been altered at three different periods: on the left is Henry VIII's Great Hall; on the opposite side of the courtyard is a gateway with the date 1732. It was built by George II, who had some alterations made. On the right is the graceful stone colonnade of Sir Christopher Wren, which leads to the entrance to the State Apartments.

90. HAMPTON COURT PALACE: THE KING'S GREAT STAIRCASE

One of the grandest staircases in England, designed by Wren as the principal approach to William III's State Rooms. The walls and ceiling were painted as one great composition by the Italian artist Antonio Verrio, about 1700. Verrio's pretentious and gaudy style triumphed in the reigns of Charles II, James II, William and Mary and Anne. The illustration shows the south wall on which are depicted Mercury dictating to Julian the Apostate, and above the door, a Roman funeral pyre. The realistic effect of the painted columns and pilasters is remarkable. The wrought-iron balustrading is by Jean Tijou, a Huguenot who settled in England.

91. HAMPTON COURT PALACE: FOUNTAIN COURT

George II's gateway leads to the colonnaded Fountain Court of William III's part of the Palace, built by Wren. The white Portland stone forms a beautiful contrast to the red brickwork, and the carved wreaths round the circular windows of the second storey give a baroque touch.

92-3. HAMPTON COURT PALACE: CHAPEL ROYAL

The magnificent fan-vaulted wooden ceiling, with its carved and gilded ribs and pendants with cherubs (plate 93) and blue vault powdered with stars, was added by Henry VIII in 1535; the chapel itself was built by Cardinal Wolsey. The altar was designed by Sir Christopher Wren for Queen Anne, and was carved by Grinling Gibbons.

94-6. CHISWICK PARK

Chiswick House (1730) was built by the third Earl of Burlington and William Kent in imitation of the Villa Almerigo at Vicenza, one of Palladio's best works. The wings were added by James Wyatt about 1792.

The grounds were laid out by William Kent and Bridgeman between 1715 and 1736. Chiswick Park was one of the first irregular gardens in Europe – as opposed to the formal symmetrical garden (such as Hampton Court) – and it is the most picturesque park in London, with cedar trees, temples (plate 96), pavilions, urns, sphinxes (plate 94), and statues from Hadrian's Villa. The bridge (plate 95) over the miniature lake is by James Wyatt.

After Lord Burlington's death Chiswick House and Park became the property of his son-in-law, the Duke of Devonshire. In the last century it was for a time a private lunatic asylum, and in 1928 the house and grounds were bought by the local borough council, and the grounds opened as a public park. In this house Charles James Fox died in 1806 and George Canning in 1827.

ILLUSTRATIONS IN THE TEXT

WESTMINSTER ABBEY: RELIEF ON THE
MONUMENT TO BISHOP WILCOCKS

The west towers of the Abbey were completed by
Nicholas Hawksmoor during the twenty-five years
that Bishop Wilcocks was Dean of Westminster
(d. 1756). He desired this fact to be commemorated
on his monument, which was erected five years
after his death. The delightful rococo relief is by
Sir Henry Cheere, who was a pupil of Schee-
makers and became a brilliant exponent of the
Rococo in English sculpture.

FRONTISPIECE. ST. PAUL'S CATHEDRAL:
NORTH-WEST TOWER

See note on plate 7

PAGE 7. ROYAL NAVAL COLLEGE,
GREENWICH: STUCCO ORNAMEN-
TATION IN THE CHAPEL

See note on plate 67

PAGE 8. HAMPTON COURT PALACE: THE
GREAT HALL, FAN-VAULTED
CEILING OVER THE DAIS

The truly magnificent Great Hall was built by
Henry VIII to replace the smaller hall of Cardinal
Wolsey's palace. It was begun in 1531 and finished
five years later. This beautiful fanvaulted ceiling
is over the dais, which is raised one step above
the floor of the main hall and lighted by a bay
window. Here the king used to dine with his favou-
rites, while the rest of the company sat at long
tables ranged down each side of the Great Hall.

ACKNOWLEDGEMENTS

All the photographs reproduced in this book have
been taken by Helmut Gernsheim, with the ex-
ception of plate 39. At the time of taking the
photographs for this book the Chapel was under
scaffolding, and a pre-war photograph by A. F.
Kersting has been used.
Permission to reproduce a number of the author's
photographs was kindly granted by *Country Life*
(plates 36, 70) and *The Warburg Institute* (plates 1,
2, 4-7, 38, 40-49, 71, 82, 83, 89-91, 93, 96 and
the illustrations on the half-title and on page 7.)
The author wishes to thank Messrs. Swan & Edgar
for permission to take the photograph of Piccadilly Circus (plate 28) from their premises.
He would also like to record his thanks to the
co-operative young policeman who twice held up
the traffic for him at Marble Arch on a busy
Saturday afternoon.